Searchlight
BOOKS™

What Can
We Do about
Pollution?

How Can We Reduce

Fossil Fuel Pollution?

Andrea Wang

Lerner Publications ◆ Minneapolis

Content Consultant: Burtron Davis, PhD, Associate Director, University of Kentucky Center for Applied Energy Research

Lerner Publications Company
A division of Lerner Publishing Group, Inc.
241 First Avenue North
Minneapolis, MN 55401 USA

For reading levels and more information, look up this title at www.lernerbooks.com.

Library of Congress Cataloging-in-Publication Data

Wang, Andrea, author.
    How can we reduce fossil fuel pollution? / Andrea Wang.
        pages cm. — (Searchlight books. What can we do about pollution?)
    Audience: Ages 8-10.
    Audience: Grades 4 to 6.
    Includes bibliographical references and index.
    ISBN 978-1-4677-9513-5 (lb : alk. paper) — ISBN 978-1-4677-9699-6 (pb : alk. paper) — ISBN 978-1-4677-9700-9 (eb pdf)
1. Fossil fuels—Juvenile literature. 2. Air—Pollution—Juvenile literature. 3. Pollution prevention—Juvenile literature. 4. Environmental protection—Juvenile literature. I. Title.
    TP318.3.W36 2016
    333.8'2—dc23
                                      2015025909

Manufactured in the United States of America
1 – VP – 12/31/15

Contents

Chapter 1

WHAT IS FOSSIL FUEL POLLUTION?

We get energy from many types of fuel. Fossil fuels are used more than any other kind of fuel. Fossil fuels include coal, natural gas, and oil. They are formed from the remains of plants and animals that died millions of years ago. Fossil fuels are nonrenewable energy sources. That means they cannot be replaced if we use them up.

A large rig collects oil from beneath the seafloor. What must happen before the oil is ready for use?

Some coal mines are 2,000 feet (600 meters) below the ground.

Before fossil fuels can be made into energy, they must be mined, drilled, or pumped out of the ground. Then they must be cleaned and prepared for use. These are dirty processes that create pollution.

Fossil fuels are then burned in power plants, homes, and vehicles. Burning these fuels produces heat and gases, which are then used to make different forms of energy. But making energy also creates pollution.

THE EXHAUST FROM A TRAIN'S SMOKESTACK IS AN EXAMPLE OF A POLLUTING GAS.

Types of Fossil Fuel Pollution

There are three main types of fossil fuel pollution. The first is solid wastes. These are the materials left behind when fossil fuels are burned. The second is wastewater. This is the water left over when fossil fuels are cleaned and prepared for use. The third is air emissions. These are the gases released when fossil fuels are burned.

Each type of pollution has effects on our environment. But people are working on solutions that can reduce their impact. You can help too!

Large pumps are used to bring oil out of the ground.

Chapter 2

SOLID WASTES

Coal and oil must be collected and prepared before they can be used. But these activities create unwanted materials called solid wastes. Despite the name, these materials are not always solid. They can also be partly solid or even liquid. The form depends on the fuel. It also depends on the cleaning processes that are used.

Coal mining results in many tons of solid waste. What other processes create solid wastes?

Digging coal out of the ground creates clouds of dust. The chunks of coal that come out of the mine also contain rocks and dirt. Water with special chemicals is then used to wash the coal. This process produces sludge. Coal sludge is a mud-like mixture. It contains water, chemicals, and small pieces of earth. Sludge and dust also contain metals such as arsenic, lead, and mercury.

A coal preparation plant washes and crushes the coal so that it is ready to be used.

An oil refinery is a plant where oil is made into useful products. There are more than 130 oil refineries in the United States.

Oil that has been pumped out of the ground also contains unwanted substances. These include sulfur, nitrogen, and metals. After those have been removed, the oil is separated into different products such as gasoline, propane, and jet fuel. This process is called refining. Refining produces solid and gaseous wastes.

Coal and oil are burned in power plants. This process generates heat and electricity. But the fuels are not completely used up when they are burned. Bottom ash and boiler slag, a melted form of coal ash, are left behind. Ash and slag contain metals such as arsenic, cadmium, and mercury. All of these leftover materials are considered solid waste.

Tiny particles of ash, called fly ash, float up through the smokestacks of power plants. The particles are caught by special filters.

People use huge amounts of fossil fuel to make electricity. In the United States alone, 4.6 billion pounds (2 billion kilograms) of coal are used every day. This generates about 40 percent of the country's electricity. Other fossil fuels are used to generate another 28 percent. Every day, making electricity creates millions of pounds of solid waste.

Every day, about 14 pounds of coal are burned for each person in the United States.

These holding areas are called surface impoundments.

What's So Bad about Solid Waste?

The chemicals and metals in solid wastes can be toxic, or poisonous. That means ash, slag, and sludge must be disposed of carefully. Wastes that are dry are usually buried in landfills. Sludgy wastes are kept in large holding areas that look like ponds. The solids settle to the bottom of the ponds. The water at the top is drained or evaporates. Sometimes the dried sludge is removed and taken to landfills. Other times the holding area is capped with clean soil and left in place. Sludge can also be poured into old coal mines for storage.

Problems occur when solid wastes get into the environment. They may leak out of landfills and holding areas. When this happens, they drain into groundwater and surface water. People who eat food or drink water polluted by these wastes can become sick. Arsenic and cadmium cause cancer. Mercury affects the human nervous system and growth.

After a solid waste leak, polluted water and soil must be removed and cleaned.

Wind can blow dry particles onto soil, plants, and animals. Breathing contaminated dust causes lung diseases such as asthma. When it rains, the water moves chemicals from solid waste particles to soil and groundwater. There, the chemicals can be taken up by plant roots. Metals such as lead can prevent seeds and plants from growing.

PEOPLE WITH ASTHMA OFTEN HAVE TO USE INHALERS. THESE DEVICES SEND MEDICATIONS INTO THE LUNGS.

IN 2008, A HOLDING AREA IN TENNESSEE SPILLED. THE ACCIDENT CAUSED DAMAGE TO MANY NEARBY HOMES.

Walls of holding areas sometimes collapse. This spills sludge into rivers or onto land. Floods of toxic sludge can destroy or poison habitats.

What Can We Do about Solid Waste?

As long as people burn fossil fuels, we will have solid waste. But we need to keep solid waste from harming the environment. Landfills and holding areas need leak-proof liners. Holding areas should be made with materials strong enough to contain the lakes of sludge.

Wind power creates electricity without producing solid waste.

Congress has the power to make environmental laws. The president has the power to make sure people follow these laws.

In 2014, the US government made a rule that required coal-burning power plants to have strong, leak-proof disposal areas. The rule also required power plants to create websites. The websites must show that the plant is disposing of coal ash properly. That way, people can see whether the power plants are following the rules.

Some solid waste from fossil fuels can be recycled. Ash can be used to make concrete and bricks. Oil sludge can be reused in the refinery.

Furnaces that burn fossil fuel should be kept in good working order. If you have this kind of furnace, ask your parents to have a technician tune it up. This will make the furnace more efficient. It will burn less fuel and make less pollution.

Oil sludge can be used to make asphalt and tar.

Chapter 3

WASTEWATER

It takes several steps to produce energy from fossil fuels. Water is used in many of these steps. It is used to clean coal. It is used in power plants to produce steam and keep machinery cool. And it is used to drill for oil and natural gas.

Water is used in power plants. Where else is it used?

Water is used to get natural gas out of tiny gaps in rocks deep underground. This process is called fracking. Water and chemicals are forced down a deep, tube-like well and into rock. The high pressure created by the liquid breaks the rock. This allows natural gas to flow out of the rock more easily.

This fracking machine forces water underground to push out natural gas.

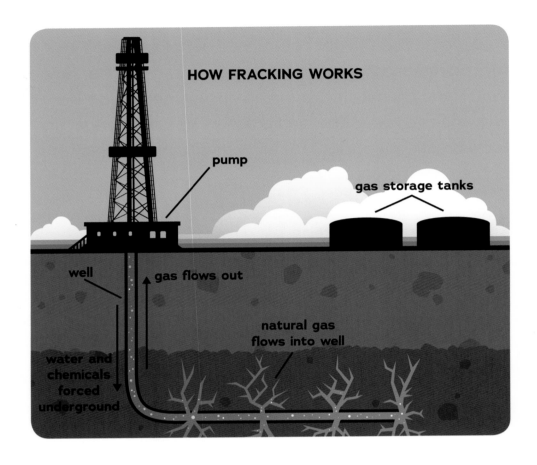

HOW FRACKING WORKS

pump

gas storage tanks

well

gas flows out

natural gas flows into well

water and chemicals forced underground

Where does all this water come from? Usually, it is pumped out of the ground. It can also come from nearby rivers and streams. When used for cooling, the water actually becomes cleaner. But it is much warmer than before. Water used for other reasons often becomes polluted with oil, salts, metals, and other materials. This dirty wastewater is sometimes piped back into lakes and rivers. It can also be pumped deep underground.

TOXIC CHEMICALS MAY CAUSE PLANTS TO GROW MORE SLOWLY. THEY CAN EVEN CAUSE PLANTS TO DIE.

What Problems Does Wastewater Cause?

The toxic chemicals in wastewater can harm the health of aquatic plants and animals. The chemicals can also flow into groundwater. In many areas, people's drinking water comes from groundwater. Drinking contaminated water can cause cancer and other health problems.

The higher temperature of wastewater can also change aquatic habitats. Hotter water holds less oxygen. Many fish species cannot live in water with low oxygen levels. So, fish start to die off when the water gets too warm.

THESE FISH DIED AFTER HOT WASTEWATER CHANGED THE TEMPERATURE OF THEIR HABITAT.

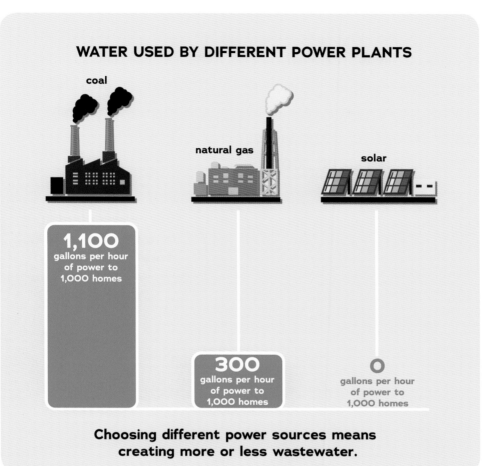

WATER USED BY DIFFERENT POWER PLANTS

coal

natural gas

solar

1,100 gallons per hour of power to 1,000 homes

300 gallons per hour of power to 1,000 homes

0 gallons per hour of power to 1,000 homes

Choosing different power sources means creating more or less wastewater.

How Can We Reduce Wastewater Pollution?

Scientists have developed new methods to clean wastewater. They may shock wastewater with electricity. This makes pollutants clump together for easy removal. They then use filters with tiny holes to remove the smallest of particles from the water.

These technologies allow oil and gas companies to recycle their wastewater. The cleaned wastewater can be used again instead of being released into the environment. As a result, the companies pump less water from rivers and lakes. This means more water for plants, animals, and people.

This power plant has its own wastewater treatment facility.

Algae often looks like a layer of green slime on the surface of the water.

Look for signs of polluted water bodies in your town. Dead fish and too much algae are two examples. If you see these signs, tell an adult. Many groups are working to clean up water bodies. Search on the Internet for one near you. Raise money with a bake sale and donate it to the group you choose. Or join a community cleanup event.

Chapter 4

AIR EMISSIONS

Fossil fuel use is one of the biggest sources of air pollution. Fossil fuels are used in power plants, vehicles, furnaces, and many other places. Burning fossil fuels creates gases and tiny particles. These gases and particles are called air emissions. They are released into the atmosphere. The cloud of exhaust from a vehicle is one example of air emissions.

Cars are one source of fossil fuel emissions. What are some others?

A worker checks valves
at a natural gas plant.

The pollutants in air emissions include carbon dioxide, nitrous oxide, sulfur dioxide, and methane. Natural gas is mostly made of methane. When natural gas escapes from leaky pipes, it pollutes the air too.

Why Are Air Emissions a Problem?

Air emissions do not just float away. Breathing air emissions can cause asthma and other health problems. Carbon dioxide, methane, and nitrous oxide are also greenhouse gases. These gases trap heat in the atmosphere. The buildup of greenhouse gases causes temperatures to rise. This is called global warming. And global warming contributes to climate change. Effects of climate change include melting ice caps and rising sea levels.

Melting ice caps cause sea levels to rise. This could cause flooding in many coastal cities.

A WORKER CLEANS A STATUE THAT HAS BEEN DAMAGED BY ACID RAIN.

Air emissions can combine in the atmosphere. When sulfur dioxide reacts with oxygen and water vapor in the air, it forms sulfuric acid. This creates acid rain that falls back to Earth. Acid rain harms forests and aquatic animals.

Steam comes out of a scrubber tower, while harmful emissions stay inside.

How Can We Reduce Air Emissions?

Power plants use "scrubbers" to trap emissions before they get into the air. They use special chemicals to break down pollutants. They can also buy new equipment that produces fewer emissions and does not leak.

Gasoline-powered vehicles produce a lot of air emissions. So, walk or ride your bike whenever you can. If you have to use a vehicle, carpool with friends or take public transportation. You can also plant a tree. Trees store carbon dioxide naturally!

Riding a bike is not only better for the environment. It's also great exercise.

Chapter 5

WE CAN MAKE A DIFFERENCE

Fossil fuel pollution is a complicated problem. It can harm animals, people, and the environment in many ways. But we can reduce fossil fuel pollution by switching to renewable energy sources. These include sunlight, wind, and water.

Rooftop solar panels create energy without burning fossil fuels. What are some other ways to create renewable energy?

Most renewable energy sources create less pollution than fossil fuels do. If more people used renewable energy, it would lower the amount of pollution. Fewer plants and animals would be harmed. Releasing fewer greenhouse gases may even slow the rate of climate change.

Hydroelectric plants use flowing water to generate power. This is a renewable energy source.

Another way to reduce fossil fuel pollution is to use less energy. Turn off the lights when you leave a room. Turn off and unplug electrical devices when you are not using them. Ask your parents to use energy-saving LED lightbulbs.

In the winter, wear a sweater instead of turning up the heat. In the summer, try not to use the air conditioner as much. Take shorter showers. Wash clothes in cold water.

LED lighbulbs use much less energy than standard bulbs. Over time, they can also help you save money.

Talk to your family and friends about how they can use less fossil fuel energy. You can also write letters to Congress. Tell them why you care about fossil fuel pollution. Your letter could help convince them to create new rules. And that could lead to a brighter future for everyone!

You can ask Congress to vote for rules that decrease the amount of pollution allowed to get into the environment.

Glossary

acid rain: rain that is more acidic than normal due to air pollution and other environmental factors

asthma: a disease of the respiratory system that makes it hard to breathe. Other symptoms include wheezing, coughing, and shortness of breath.

boiler slag: a material that is left over after coal is burned

coal: a hard, solid fossil fuel formed underground from the remains of plants and animals

dispose: to throw away or get rid of something

fossil fuel: coal, petroleum, natural gas, or other fuel formed when plant or animal remains are subjected to high heat and pressure over time

groundwater: water that has sunk into the earth and collected in the spaces between soil and rock particles

nonrenewable: something that cannot be made, grown, or reused quickly enough to keep up with demand

particle: a tiny bit or piece of a substance

renewable: something that can be created, grown, or reused very quickly so that it does not run out

sludge: a mud-like mixture of solid and liquid waste

Learn More about Fossil Fuel Pollution

Books

Doeden, Matt. *Finding Out about Coal, Oil, and Natural Gas.* Minneapolis: Lerner, 2015. Interesting facts and colorful photos take readers into the world of energy production.

Flounders, Anne. *Power for the Planet.* South Egremont, MA: Red Chair Press, 2014. This fascinating book explores how we get our energy and how we can cause less pollution.

Spilsbury, Richard, and Louise Spilsbury. *Fossil Fuel Power.* New York: PowerKids Press, 2012. This book helps readers understand the costs and benefits of using fossil fuels.

Websites

Energy Quest
http://www.energyquest.ca.gov/
This interactive site features lots of great information on energy use.

Energy Star Kids
http://www.energystar.gov/index.cfm?c=kids.kids_index
Find out how you can make a difference on this colorful website.

Recycle City
http://www3.epa.gov/recyclecity/index.htm
Games and activities make this site a fun way to learn about recycling.

Index

Photo Acknowledgments

The images in this book are used with the permission of: © Darryl Peroni/iStockphoto, p. 4; © Alex Potemkin/iStockphoto, p. 5; © remik44992/Shutterstock Images, p. 6; © hanhanpeggy/iStockphoto, p. 7; © hsvrs/iStockphoto, p. 8; © Cuhrig/iStockphoto, p. 9; © Anton Foltin/Shutterstock Images, p. 10; © ppart/iStockphoto, p. 11; © Libor Polansky/iStockphoto/Thinkstock, p. 12; © Andrew Harrer/ Bloomberg/Getty Images, p. 13; © Sam Riche/Lexington Herald-Leader/AP Images, p. 14; © CT757fan/iStockphoto, p. 15; © Wade Payne/AP Images, p. 16; © gyn9038/iStockphoto, p. 17; © Lawrence Jackson/White House, p. 18; © jocic/iStockphoto/Thinkstock, p. 19; © Cardaf/ Shutterstock Images, p. 20; © Doran J. Clark/iStockphoto, p. 21; © filo/iStockphoto, p. 22; © Rainer von Brandis/iStockphoto, p. 23; © Opgrapher/Shutterstock Images, p. 24; © Its design/ Shutterstock Images, p. 25 (left), 25 (center), 25 (right); © John Kasawa/iStockphoto, p. 26; © Luis Santos/Shutterstock Images, p. 27; © Ralph125/iStockphoto, p. 28; © Budimir Jevtic/Shutterstock Images, p. 29; © florianwirsing/iStockphoto, p. 30; © Matt Rourke/AP Images, p. 31; © TFoxFoto/ Shutterstock Images, p. 32; © Michael Jung/Shutterstock Images, p. 33; © Smileus/Shutterstock Images, p. 34; © Samo Trebizan/Shutterstock Images, p. 35; © koosen/Shutterstock Images, p. 36; © Gelpi JM/Shutterstock Images, p. 37.

Front Cover: © pand demin/Shutterstock Images

Main body text set in Adrianna Regular 14/20.
Typeface provided by Chank.